W9-BFA-415

FOCUS ON FAMILY MATTERS

Understanding and Coping with Divorce

FOCUS ON FAMILY MATTERS

The Blending of Foster and Adopted Children into the Family

Dealing with Terminal Illness in the Family

Dealing with the Effects of Rape and Incest

The Effects of Job Loss on the Family

Teen Pregnancy

Understanding and Coping with Divorce

Focus on Family Matters

Understanding and Coping with Divorce

Media Center
MacArthur Middle School
Rockenbach Road
Ft. Meade, Md. 20755

Heather Lehr Wagner

Marvin Rosen, Ph.D.
Consulting Editor

Chelsea House Publishers
Philadelphia

CHELSEA HOUSE PUBLISHERS

EDITOR IN CHIEF Sally Cheney
DIRECTOR OF PRODUCTION Kim Shinners
CREATIVE MANAGER Takeshi Takahashi
MANUFACTURING MANAGER Diann Grasse

Staff for UNDERSTANDING AND COPING WITH DIVORCE

ASSOCIATE EDITOR Bill Conn
PICTURE RESEARCHER Sarah Bloom
PRODUCTION ASSISTANT Jaimie Winkler
SERIES DESIGNER Takeshi Takahashi
LAYOUT 21st Century Publishing and Communications, Inc.

http://www.chelseahouse.com

First Printing

1 3 5 7 9 8 6 4 2

Library of Congress Cataloging-in-Publication Data

Wagner, Heather Lehr.
    Understanding and coping with divorce / by Heather Lehr Wagner.
        p. cm. — (Focus on family matters)
    Includes bibliographical references and index.
    ISBN 0-7910-6691-6
        1. Children of divorced parents. 2. Divorce. 3. Teenagers—Family relationships.
    4. Parent and teenager. I. Title. II. Series.
HQ777.5.W33 2002
306.89—dc21
                                                                    2001008122

Contents

	Introduction	6
1	Dealing with Divorce	8
2	And They Lived Happily Ever After	14
3	Custody and Visitation	24
4	The Single Parent Challenge	34
5	Step-by-Step to a New Family	40
6	A New Start	48
	Glossary	60
	Further Reading	61
	Index	62

Introduction

Marvin Rosen, Ph.D.
Consulting Editor

B ad things sometimes happen to good people. We've probably all heard that expression. But what happens when the "good people" are teenagers?

Growing up is stressful and difficult to negotiate. Teenagers are struggling to becoming independent, trying to cut ties with their families that they see as restrictive, burdensome, and unfair. Rather than attempting to connect in new ways with their parents, they may withdraw. When bad things do happen, this separation may make the teen feel alone in coping with difficult and stressful issues.

Focus on Family Matters provides teens with practical information about how to cope when bad things happen to them. The series deals foremost with feelings—the emotional pain associated with adversity. Grieving, fear, anger, stress, guilt, and sadness are addressed head on. Teens will gain valuable insight and advice about dealing with their feelings, and for seeking help when they cannot help themselves.

The authors in this series identify some of the more serious problems teens face. In so doing, they make three assumptions: First, teens who find themselves in difficult situations are not at fault and should not blame themselves. Second, teens can overcome difficult situations, but may need help to do so. Third, teens bond with their families, and the strength of this bond influences their ability to handle difficult situations.

These books are also about communication—specifically about the value of communication. None of the problems covered occurs in a vacuum, and none of the situations should be faced by anyone alone. Each either involves a close family member or affects the entire family. Since families teach teens how to trust, relate to others, and solve problems, teens need to bond with families to develop normally and become emotionally whole. Success in dealing with adversity depends not only on the strength of the individual teen, but also upon the resources of the family in providing support, advice, and material assistance. Strong attachment to care givers in a supporting, nurturing, safe family structure is essential to successful coping.

Some teens learn to cope with adversity—they absorb the pain, they adjust, and they go on. But for others, the trauma they experience seems like an insurmountable challenge—they become angry, stressed, and depressed. They may withdraw from friends, they may stop going to school, and their grades may slip. They may draw negative attention to themselves and express their pain and fear by rebelling. Yet, in each case, healing can occur.

The teens who cope well with adversity, who are able to put the past behind them and regain their momentum, are no less sensitive or caring than those who suffer most. Yet there is a difference. Teens who are more resilient to trauma are able to dig deep down into their own resources, to find strength in their families and in their own skills, accomplishments, goals, aspirations, and values. They are able to find reasons for optimism and to feel confidence in their capabilities. This series recognizes the effectiveness of these strategies, and presents problem-solving skills that every teen can use.

Focus on Family Matters is positive, optimistic, and supportive. It gives teens hope and reinforces the power of their own efforts to handle adversity. And most importantly, it shows teens that while they cannot undo the bad things that have happen, they have the power to shape their own futures and flourish as healthy, productive adults.

Dealing with Divorce

■ Every Friday afternoon, Amanda packs a small bag with clothes, CDs and anything else she will need for the weekend. By 6:00 p.m., her bag is next to the door and she is waiting at the window, watching for her father's car. He is hardly ever on time, but Amanda knows that if she isn't there to open the door her mother will be, and her parents will have a fight. Her parents have been divorced for five years, and she spends weekdays with her mother and weekends with her father and stepmother. In their separate homes, with their separate lives, her mother and father behave normally, but whenever they are together they get into an argument almost immediately. It is impossible for Amanda to imagine that they once loved each other enough to get married in the first place.

Divorce means something different for every person who experiences it. But in every case, children must find a way to cope with how their parents' divorce will change the way they think about their family and themselves. They will need to

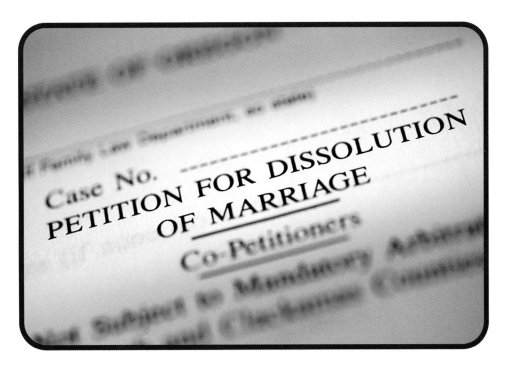

Divorce brings the lawyers and judges into what were once private family matters. It is important to remember that divorce does not break the bonds of caring between parents and children.

accept that the reality of their family life may be quite different from how they wish it would be, and yet understand that there are small steps they can take to make sure that they are not caught in the middle.

What is a divorce?

A **divorce** is a legal document that ends a marriage. Estimates suggest that as many as half of all marriages end in divorce, so it is quite likely that your parents or the parents of someone you know are divorced. While the ending of a marriage in divorce is common, the children of

> **Who decides where children will live after their parents separate?**

divorcing parents know that their situation is not predictable or even easy to understand. When a family comes apart, the one thing everyone shares is pain.

While there may be a legal document that ends a marriage, anyone involved with a divorce knows that taking apart a family is never simple or fast. There must be decisions made about **assets** (the property a husband and wife share)—things like a house, cars, furniture and other items that must be divided between the two people divorcing. Decisions must be made about finances, and frequently the legal document that spells out the divorce will contain wording about things like **alimony** (money given by the husband or wife who earns more to the spouse who doesn't, usually for a few years after the divorce is finalized) and **child support** (money given to the parent with whom the children will live to help with the children's expenses).

How does a divorce

change your family?

Finally, the divorce **decree** (the legal document spelling out the terms of the divorce) will often contain decisions about **custody**—the parent with whom the children will live, how often they will visit the other parent, and other information designed to make sure that the arrangements for the children are clear.

While a husband and wife may sometimes both agree on the decision to divorce, they may not agree on the terms—on how the money and property will be shared, and more importantly, on the decisions about their children. Generally, both parents will ask an attorney or lawyer to help them sort out these issues. This can be a painful and confusing time, both for the parents and their children, as difficult decisions are being made that will change their family.

Once the terms of the divorce have been decided, the

When a husband and wife decide to divorce, they must make tough decisions that will affect the lives of their children. This is an emotionally stressful time for any family, as issues of money, property, and child custody are decided and the responsibilities of the parents are divided.

divorce decree is filed in court and signed by a judge or other official of the court. The divorce is then considered finalized, and the marriage is officially ended.

An ending and a beginning

For any family in this situation, the divorce is an ending and a beginning—an ending of the marriage, but a beginning of new relationships and new circumstances. Some families must move into a new apartment or house because the family's home is too expensive for only one parent to maintain. A mother who had stayed home to take care of her children may find that she now needs to get a job. Parents who used to attend their children's school events together may now find it awkward and uncomfortable to be in the same place. Parents may still argue about custody or money problems, even after the divorce has been finalized.

What would you miss

if your parents were not together?

It is important to remember that the divorce ends only a marriage. The parents have chosen to divorce each other, not their children. They will always be parents even if they are no longer married to each other. A family can continue beyond a divorce, but it will take tremendous patience and effort from everyone involved to make sure that there is room in their new life for the important pieces of their life before the divorce.

In this book, we will talk about the issues surrounding divorce. We will discover some coping skills to help you avoid being caught in the middle of divorced parents. We will examine the ways divorce impacts your life—how to deal with different rules in different households and how to handle times when both parents will be together. We will look at some of the challenges you will face when a parent decides to date again, and talk about stepfamilies and how to stay sane if you're in one. Finally, we'll share some additional resources that may be helpful if you find yourself coping with divorcing or divorced parents, or helping someone who is.

Each year, more than one million children and young people in the U.S. find themselves caught in a family struggling with separation or divorce. While a divorce is

Parents may continue to argue, even after their divorce is final. Sometimes these disagreements can leave children feeling alone and isolated.

finalized and a marriage legally ended on a single day with a single document, the process of coping with divorce takes much longer. Families will find themselves confronting many challenges. Rebuilding a family will take time, but it can be done.

And They Lived Happily Ever After

When Kelly's parents told her they were getting a divorce, she did not believe them at first. They had plenty of fights, but so did all of her friends' parents. It did not make sense. They could not give her a good reason. They kept saying that they didn't love each other any more, that they wanted different things. Well, everybody changed—she was changing, her little brother was changing—but that didn't give them the right to break up the family. Did it?

Kelly was angry with her parents. They didn't seem to care how sad they made her and her brother. She thought that if they would just try harder, they could stop fighting and they would all be a happy family again.

A divorce represents the death of a marriage, and for all of the family members involved the sadness they feel is as if something important and precious to them has died. There is no point in trying to hide these feelings, or to pretend that

In a perfect world, the love a couple feels on their wedding day would last their whole lives. When this doesn't happen, children often struggle to understand why their parents can no longer live together.

everything is okay. Most parents will feel sad and disappointed when a divorce takes place, even if they had agreed to end their marriage. We all wish for happy endings, and when they don't come it can make us feel confused or angry or depressed, or sometimes all three.

A writer named Elisabeth Kübler-Ross identified five stages, or feelings, that we go through when we experience the death of someone or something important to us. The first stage is denial—you pretend that something awful isn't happening in the hope that if you ignore it, it will go away. Next comes anger—you understand this feeling if you've ever asked, "Why is this happening?" or "How could they do that to me?" The third stage is called bargaining—you try to change what's happening through your own actions. For example, you might say, "If I am really good, and get straight As and help more around the house, maybe my parents won't get divorced." The fourth stage is depression—you may feel the most helpless or hopeless. Finally, you reach the stage called acceptance—you accept that the divorce is going to happen and understand that you are not responsible for it or for trying to change your parents' actions.

These five stages—denial, anger, bargaining, depression and acceptance—are very common as family members struggle to deal with a divorce. They do not always happen clearly or neatly; you may feel sad one day and angry the next. It is like rock climbing—you may need to move sideways, or even slip back down a bit, before you can attack the climb from a new spot.

What would it feel like if your parents decided to get a divorce?

If your parents are divorcing, you should understand that all of these feelings are normal; it is right to feel them. You should feel angry and sad when your family is coming apart. There are no quick and easy ways to feel better, but sharing your feelings can help. Find someone that you feel comfortable talking to, and let him or her know what is happening. Don't feel as if you must pretend that everything is okay. About half of all marriages end in divorce, so many teens are dealing with the problems caused by divorcing or divorced parents.

If you have a friend whose parents are getting a divorce, remember that they are struggling with something terribly sad. They will need all the support and understanding you can offer.

It came out of the blue

For teenagers whose parents decide to separate, the family changes that result can be particularly painful. There is no good age to experience a parents' divorce—even for adults, a parent's decision to leave the other parent can cause tremendous sadness—but as you become a teenager, you begin the natural development that is described too

> **How would it feel**
>
> **if one of your parents decided to move out of your house?**

simply as "growing up." Adolescence can be a difficult and challenging process, as you slowly begin to sort out what your own beliefs and desires are and begin to make choices about your future. Part of this process involves a gradual separation from your parents. It may seem strange that, just at the point when you begin to separate from your parents, it can be especially difficult if they choose to separate from each other, but part of the process of shaping your own identity comes from your contact with your parents. If they are not available, or if they are caught up in their own crises, it becomes harder to feel secure as you step into adulthood.

It's as if you are an explorer, setting off into unknown territory, which is really what adulthood is. The future is unknown when you're a teen, although the choices you make, the paths you choose, will lead you onward. Like

The teenage child of divorced or separated parents faces some special challenges. The adolescent may feel insecure as she tries to establish her own identity without the joint guidance of both parents.

any explorer, you need a base camp from which to set out and return to—a place to map out your journey, to gather supplies for the trip, and to get encouragement and an understanding that you are not alone.

Your family can be this base camp for you, providing you with a solid starting point for your journey and equipping you for the trip. But if your base camp is in chaos, with people coming and going and no one able to focus, it will be difficult for you to find what you need before you set out. This is what happens when your parents decide to divorce as you start on the path to adulthood.

Is the future hopeless when this happens? Of course not. There are some steps you can take to help you feel more secure at this difficult time.

Problem solving

The first, and most important, thing to remember when your parents decide to separate or divorce is that it is *their* decision, based on their feelings about *each other*. Too often the children of divorcing parents believe that they are somehow responsible, that something they did or said has caused the parents to end the marriage. This is simply not true. When adults talk about their reasons for leaving a marriage, the reasons generally center on their feelings

Are you to blame

if your parents decide to divorce?

about themselves and each other, not the actions of their children. Just as it was the two parents, not their children, who chose to begin the marriage based on their feelings for each other, it is these same two people (and only them) who are responsible for the feelings and actions that caused the marriage to end.

Why is it important to remember this? Because the kind of thinking that may lead you to believe that something you did or said caused your parents to separate may also lead you to think that your actions or words may be all that are needed to get your parents back together. Believing something like, "If I get straight As, my mom won't want to divorce my dad," or "If I just stay out of his way and don't ask him for things, my dad won't be so tired and sad and won't want to leave," only sets you up for disappointment when your actions don't bring your parents back together.

It is sad but true that, despite what they say in fairy tales, two people who fall in love do not always live happily ever after. But while romantic love—the love that starts a marriage in the first place—can fade or disappear, the love parents have for their children is quite different and much more lasting. A parent's decision to leave the marriage does not mean that he or she is choosing to leave the children. However, as adults think about separation

Can you do anything to make your parents stay together?

and divorce, they are generally focused more on themselves and each other than on their children. As they spend time talking—or arguing—about what they want to do, they may not appreciate how shocking and unexpected these plans can be for their children.

While you may not be able to change your parents' decisions, it is certainly okay to let them know how you feel. If you are confused, or upset, or angry, let them know that you don't understand. Ask them to explain, as best they can, what is happening and what they expect to happen in the future. Ask them to share their plans with you. If a parent decides to leave, ask them to commit to a day when they will visit, or a regular time to call.

Too often we waste time denying or being embarrassed about our feelings, pretending that we are not sad or angry or confused. Parents should expect that their decision to divorce will leave many questions that need to be answered, and they should be prepared to answer at least some of those questions. But if you feel uncomfortable sharing your feelings with your parents, find someone that you can talk to—a counselor, a friend, a family member, or other adult you trust.

Divorce only ends the marriage, not the love that parents feel for their children. Yet, parents may not always appreciate the shock and pain their children feel when the family is forced to change.

As nearly half of all marriages end in divorce, you should understand that many, many teens are struggling with the same questions and concerns. We will talk about more of these questions and concerns in the chapters that follow, and share some resources at the end of this book that may help you.

Caught in the middle

Often, in the earliest stages of a divorce, the two parents can be quite angry, placing blame for the end of the marriage on each other, openly criticizing each other, or

When a couple is in the midst of a divorce, it may be tough for their children not to feel "caught in the middle" as they struggle with the desire to bridge the gap between their parents.

worse, refusing to speak to each other and asking the children to carry messages back and forth. One of the most important pieces of advice this book can give you is this: DO NOT BE CAUGHT IN THE MIDDLE!

What does it mean to be "caught in the middle"? It

means trying to serve as a bandage—holding your parents together by bridging the gap between them. It means becoming a messenger—carrying information and comments back and forth between two parents who are refusing to speak to each other. It means choosing sides by backing one parent or the other.

How would you feel

if one of your parents started criticizing the other?

These are some of the nasty roles that children can try to fill when their parents decide to divorce, and it is important to try to avoid playing any of them. While you may ultimately live with only one of your parents after the divorce is finalized, you will want to spend time with both of them. There is no right or wrong side in a divorce, only two sides that, sadly, have decided not to come together.

If a parent asks you to carry a message to the other parent, you can politely say that you would prefer that they talk to each other rather than through you. If a parent begins to criticize the other parent, simply tell them that it makes you sad to hear them say those things. Don't try to be the referee in their fights, or try to negotiate bringing them back together.

Custody and Visitation

■ Amanda is one teen wrestling with the reality of things like custody and visitation. She lives with her mother, but spends every weekend with her father and stepmother. She has her own room and clothes in each home, so she only needs to pack a small bag to go from one home to the other. She spends a few weeks with each parent during the summer, and alternates holidays every year, so that one year she might celebrate Thanksgiving with her father and Christmas with her mother, and the next year they switch.

"My friends think I'm so lucky," Amanda says. "They think that I get twice as much of everything, because I have two Christmases and two birthdays. I suppose that it's okay for those two days, but the rest of the time it isn't. I'm always forgetting homework or school books, and my mom and dad both get mad if they have to drive me back to the other house. And I'm homesick a lot. Sometimes if I'm at my dad's I can't wait to be back at my mom's, and sometimes at my mom's I just miss my dad so much."

In a divorce, the legal terms of "custody" and "visitation" determine where the children of divorced parents live and when the absent parent gets to see the children.

There are many different ways in which divorcing parents can decide to spend time with their children. When decisions are made about which parent will be responsible for their child—and when they will have that responsibility—the term **custody** is used. Custody involves the legal right to take care of someone, and to be responsible for making the decisions that will affect him or her. When a parent is said to have custody of his or her children, this means that the children live primarily with that parent, and that parent will be in charge of making the important decisions that will affect the child on a daily basis—decisions about their health care, their education, and other matters. The children may still spend time with and visit their other parent, but the parent with whom they live will be the one making most of the decisions about their care.

In some cases, parents share **joint custody**. This means that the parents who are divorcing or divorced agree to share responsibility for the care of their children, making decisions together about important matters. In cases where parents share custody, their children generally spend time with both parents, perhaps living with one parent during the week and another on weekends, or spending a few weeks in one parent's home before moving to the other's.

To make sure that both parents get to spend time with their child, regardless of who has custody, a schedule of **visitation** is often created when parents divorce. This document spells out exactly when and for how long children will visit each parent, whether on a single day, every other weekend, or for summers and holidays.

Problem solving

Often the most difficult part of moving back and forth between two parents' homes comes when the visit first begins. Even when parents have been divorced for some time, they still can become irritated or upset when they see their former husband or wife. They may also feel sad or anxious about their child leaving, even if it's only for a few days or a few hours. This can make their child feel guilty or worried about leaving.

What would it feel like to go back and forth between two homes, living part of the time with your mother and part of the time with your father?

It's important to remember that both parents need to spend time with their child, and that once the visit has been agreed to or written down in a legal document, everyone should stick to what has been scheduled. In this way, both parents can feel comfortable that they will each spend time with their child. Any discussion about the schedule or length of visits should be agreed to well before a parent comes to pick up their son or daughter.

You can help by making sure that you know when you are scheduled to visit your mother or father, and making sure that you are ready at that time. Ask your parents to mark up a calendar with scheduled visits and holidays—or mark up one yourself. Keep the calendar in a handy place so that, when school activities or sports practices are scheduled, you'll know if you will need to ask your parent to arrange a different pick-up time or place.

What about when parents are late to pick up their child for a visit? It's important to remember that anyone can get caught in traffic, that cars or transportation can be unreliable, and that sometimes people can be unexpectedly delayed. But if a parent is almost always late, or frequently calls at the last minute to postpone a visit, it's important to be honest and let them know that the visit and the schedule are important to you. They may need to change their pick-up time because of work demands or other problems. If everyone can stick to the schedule whenever possible, but be flexible about occasional conflicts, the beginning of each visit should be much smoother.

> ## How would it feel
>
> **if your mom or dad came late or forgot to pick you up when you were supposed to visit them?**

The At-Home Bag

It can be difficult to move back and forth between parents. Some teens are lucky enough to have their own space when they visit each parent, while others carry clothes and belongings back and forth. No matter whether you visit both parents frequently, or live with one and only see the other from time to time, it's important to feel "at home" wherever you are.

One good idea is to carry an **At-Home Bag**. This can be a backpack, a duffle bag, or a small paper or plastic bag where you keep a few things that will instantly make you feel at home. It may hold CDs, a stuffed animal, or a new book you're reading. You may want to keep a football in it, or some pictures, or your favorite T-shirt. The important thing is to make sure that you always have one or two special things that can help keep you at home no matter whose home you're in, things that don't belong to "Mom's place" or "Dad's place," but rather will be with you no matter where you are.

Different rules for different places

Moving from classroom to classroom in school, you can see how different teachers expect their students to follow different rules. Some teachers may be very strict and expect students to be completely silent in their classroom, while others may encourage students to interrupt or ask questions. Some may assign more homework, while others show movies or play music, and still others terrorize students with frequent pop quizzes.

Just as there are many different teaching styles, there are even more styles of parenting. When parents are divorced, they may choose to cooperate and exercise the same rules in both homes but, more commonly, each parent will make different decisions about rules and discipline. One parent may want all homework to be finished before the television is turned on. Another may set an earlier bedtime for school nights. There may be different chores to be done, different rules about going out with friends or using the telephone, and differences about what television shows or movies are acceptable.

> **What would you do**
>
> **if your parents could not agree on an important decision that affected you?**

In some cases, each parent may have different religious beliefs, or one parent may hold more conservative views about what their child should wear, whether or not they can date, or whether or not they can wear jewelry or makeup. Even the most basic routines—when everyone wakes up or goes to bed, when meals are served (and what kind of food they contain)—can vary greatly from one household to the other.

It can be very challenging, both for parents and their children, to adjust to these different expectations. At heart, parents are simply trying to make decisions about what is best for their children, but these decisions may be quite different in their different homes. In the same way that a school contains a basic set of expectations and certain basic codes of behavior for each student, but each teacher has his or her own rules for the class, divorced parents generally share a broad agreement about wanting their children to be safe, successful, and happy. But they may choose very different ways to accomplish that goal.

The Big Events

Most custody and visitation agreements schedule regular time with each parent, and often include arrangements for holidays and vacations. But there are many important days that are left unscheduled—things like birthdays, school concerts, or sports events—which both parents may want to share.

You may feel differently about these events when they involve divorced parents. For large gatherings, where there will be a crowd of people present (things like football games, graduations, or school plays), you may feel quite comfortable and even happy to have both parents present and sharing in the special day. But for smaller gatherings, like a birthday party, Christmas dinner, or other family reunion, you may feel anxious or uncomfortable if both parents are together.

It's important to remember that, just as each situation is different, people's reactions can be quite different. It is probably best and easiest to invite both parents to special events, letting them know that you have invited the other parent, as well. Don't allow yourself to be caught in the middle and trust

Holidays, birthdays, and other major events may require special scheduling arrangements for divorced parents. Sharing time at these occasions may mean that you see one parent at Christmas, another on your birthday.

the adults to behave themselves! If problems have cropped up at past events, you could always say something respectful but straightforward like, "I've invited both you and Mom to my game. I know you understand that I want you both to share this with me. It embarrasses me when you argue in front of other people, so why don't you sit in a different section? I'll look for you after the game, and we can talk then."

This kind of conversation takes care of several problems. You let your parents know that they both are important to you, and you want them to be with you for special events. It also reminds them to behave themselves since it upsets you when they get into fights. Finally, it lets them know that they can keep their distance from the other parent, because you will find them and talk to them after the event.

What would you do

if both parents wanted to spend your birthday with you?

Birthdays can be another source of stress when both parents want to celebrate your birth and share the special day with you. If your parents get along well, you may feel quite comfortable having a party where both are present. Alternatively, it may be more comfortable to celebrate your birthday with whatever parent you are with on that day, and plan to celebrate with the other parent when you are next with them. And the hidden benefit of this is you get to celebrate your birthday twice!

Where do I want to be?

When children are small, or when a divorce is first finalized, decisions are made about where the children should live based on the situation at that time. A mother or father may be better able to handle their children's needs at one particular time, but as everyone grows and changes, these circumstances may also change.

Should teens be able to choose which parent they want to live with? The answer should be "yes," but more often the correct answer is "maybe." Why?

Decisions about custody are often the result of difficult negotiations between divorcing parents. A legal arrangement may be made after complicated discussions by lawyers, or after a judge or other representative of the court has considered what is best for the children involved. One parent may be better able to provide a stable, safe environment for their

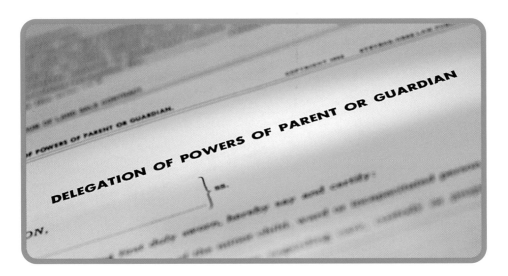

You may not always be able to choose how much time you spend with each of your parents—or even which parent you live with. Lawyers, judges, and the law often have a lot to say about where and when children get to see their parents after a divorce.

children. Factors that influence these decisions include things like whether or not a parent is able to provide financially for the children, with enough money for food, clothing, and housing. A parent's work situation may require long hours on the job, frequent moves, or lengthy absences, making it difficult for them to take care of their children, keep them in school, and otherwise supervise them. A parent may be dealing with addictions, and will need to get well and healthy before being able to take care of his or her children.

There are many reasons why a decision may be made to give custody of the children to one parent or the other, but many of these are temporary circumstances that may change over time. In addition, many courts feel that very young children are better placed with their mother,

Should you be allowed to choose which parent you live with?

although this is no longer always the case.

As children grow into teens, as jobs or financial situations change, and as parents rebuild their lives and make new choices, everyone may decide that a new custody arrangement must be agreed upon. A teenage boy who has been raised by his mother may decide that he would like to live with his father. A divorced mother may move closer to her ex-husband and their children may wish to spend equal time in both homes, rather than living principally with one parent and seeing the other only on weekends.

There are many different possibilities, but the basic reasons for the initial decision must be studied first. Was the decision made because the children were young and needed more supervision? If so, it may make sense to rethink the arrangement when the children are older, in school, and better able to take care of themselves when a parent is working. Was the decision made for financial reasons? A parent may have obtained a better-paying job, or may now have an apartment or home with room for the children to live.

In all of these cases, it is best to be open and honest. If you would like to live with another parent, talk to them first. Let them know what you are thinking, and ask them for their thoughts. While it may not be practical or possible to completely change the custody arrangement right away, it may be possible to increase the length of your visits, possibly adding on a Friday afternoon to a weekend visit, or staying for a week during holidays or summers.

While your wishes should matter, it is ultimately up to your parents to sort out the final arrangements, just as they did when the divorce first was finalized. It may need to be handled legally, or the parents may be able to negotiate a sensible arrangement between themselves. While you can and should let your wishes be known, it will in the end be up to your parents to decide what they think will be best for you.

The Single Parent Challenge

Jack's parents have been divorced since he was three years old, and no matter how hard he tries, he cannot remember what his family was like when they were all together. His father calls him on Christmas Eve and on his birthday (although sometimes he misses by a day or two), and he lives hundreds of miles away. Jack has seen him a few times during summer visits to his grandparents, but it was awkward, as if they were strangers, and his father never stayed for more than a few hours. Jack has never seen where his father lives. His father has never seen him play football. They share a name, but not much more.

There are times when a parent chooses not to be actively involved in their child's life. This can be one of the saddest results of a divorce. For some adults, divorce represents a failure—a failure to make a marriage work, a failure to be a good husband or wife—and this can be extremely painful to accept. For parents who feel this failure especially strongly, they may be

Suddenly living in a single-parent home can give rise to some painful feelings. Learning to cope with these emotions is a valuable skill, but it takes time.

embarrassed to think about the reasons why the marriage didn't work, and their own actions that may have contributed to the end of the marriage.

This sense of shame and failure may be so strong that these parents feel unable to deal with it. They may choose to avoid facing their failure by avoiding any evidence that it happened, and this often means that they choose not to see their children.

There are other reasons why a parent may not be able to be actively involved in a child's life after a divorce. For financial reasons, such as a job change, a need to find work, or a desire to save money, one or both parents may move away and the distance may make visits difficult. A parent may have a job that involves frequent travel or frequent moves, making it hard to schedule regular time with their children.

No matter what the reason, it can be quite difficult to understand why a parent would choose not to spend time with his or her child. Generally, these parents love their children and believe, incorrectly, that they are somehow making it easier or better for them by staying away. At times, one parent may make it difficult for the other to see the children as a way of punishing them for the divorce. Trouble may also occur when a parent is unable to pay the amount the court has ordered paid for child support. When this happens, the parent who owes money may be embarrassed and stay away, or the other parent may refuse to allow that parent to visit until the money owed has been paid.

> **How would you feel**
>
> **if your mother or father never visited you?**

It is, of course, wrong for parents to place the children in the middle of fights over money. And it is equally wrong for parents to not make the effort to spend time with their children.

Problem solving

If you are one of the many children who has a parent that chooses not to be part of their lives, the rare times you spend with your mother or father are quite painful because it makes you feel so helpless. You are unsure whether or not your absent parent will appear for an unexpected visit or how long the visit will last, and you may resent that parent for "dropping in" rather than making plans in advance so that everyone knows what to expect.

One solution you might try is to phone your mother or father to schedule a visit. The parent with whom you live, or a close relative, may be willing to help you make this call. This can make it easier for everyone to plan, and will also give you an opportunity to schedule other activities so that

Sparse contact and brief, unexpected visits may make children feel even less connected to an absent parent. Sometimes the child must take the first step, scheduling more visits and asking to be more involved in their parent's life.

you are not building up anxiety as you wait for a visit.

You may also have questions about your absent parent's life, and want them to care more about your activities and interests. One solution is to tell your parent that you would like to see

What would you do

if your mother or father did not schedule visits, but "popped in" once or twice a year?

their home, or to meet their new family. It's natural to be curious about stepbrothers and stepsisters, and seeing where your parent lives may help you to understand what their life is like. In the same way, you could share information about your activities or school.

It may seem unfair to ask you to take responsibility for

scheduling these visits, but you may choose to do so to let your parent know that you would like to get to know them better. Too often divorced parents mistakenly assume that it is somehow "easier" for their children if only one parent raises them. It is okay to let them know you disagree!

A parent comes back

What happens when a mother or father chooses not to be involved in their child's life for several years, and then suddenly reappears? Should they be allowed to step back into the picture, and if so, what rules should be set up to make sure that everyone feels comfortable with this new relationship?

As we discussed earlier, there are many reasons why a parent may step out of a child's life. As time passes, they may regret this decision, and miss their child. They may want to reestablish contact, and even visit more frequently.

What would you do

if your father or mother reappeared and wanted to spend time with you after not seeing you for several years?

A decision about whether or not to go ahead with the visit, where it should take place and how long it should last should probably be made by you and the parent who has taken on the responsibility of raising you. The important thing is to make sure that you are comfortable with whatever is decided. It is probably best to pick a place at a familiar spot, perhaps your home or a relative's home, and to decide ahead of time how long you would like to spend there for this first visit.

Everyone involved will probably feel anxious about this meeting. The important thing is to be honest with both parents. If you want to see the father you haven't seen for several years, let your mother know that. Perhaps you might let her know that simply wanting to see your father does not mean you love her any less. Or suppose it is your mother who has been gone from your life for a long time. When you first meet her, don't feel that you have to pretend that what she did was fine if you feel hurt or angry about it. Be honest with your emotions. You have a right to feel upset or confused.

While it is natural to want to spend time with both parents, it is also understandable if you do not feel ready to see a parent who has been out of your life for some time. Don't make any decision like this too quickly. Take your time, and think about what *you* really want. If you are not ready to welcome a parent back into your life, then let them know that. Tell them that you need more time.

One of the most difficult side effects of divorce is that parents frequently make choices based on what is best for them, not their children. There are a few opportunities where you can decide how to handle things in the way best for you. When a parent wants to reenter your life, you can ask them to respect your choices and to make this reunion as easy and comfortable as possible.

A parent who suddenly wants to be more involved in a child's life after a long absence can create some special pressures. At these times it is important for you to be honest with both parents about your feelings.

What would you do

if you wanted to spend more time with your mother or father?

Step-by-Step
to a New Family

■ Will's mother told him that she wants to get married again, to a man she has been dating for a few months. Will had just started to get used to all of the changes that came when his parents divorced—holidays spent with mom or dad but never both, and a schedule of visits between two homes so complicated that he needs to check the calendar once a week to make sure that he knows where he'll be the following week. But now he's getting a stepfather, and one with his own children, too. Will met them once and hated them—and now they're supposed to become his brothers?

Many teens find themselves facing the challenges of being part of a stepfamily. Even when parents have been divorced for several years, it can be quite painful to realize that they intend to marry someone else. It is normal and natural to believe that your parents will get back together, even when they have been divorced for a long time.

Building new relationships within a stepfamily can be tough, but it is an important part of creating a safe, emotionally healthy environment.

When a parent decides to marry someone else, you have to let go of the fantasy that your family will be reunited, and that can be quite difficult to do.

The awkward moments can begin when a divorced parent decides to date. You may find yourself sizing up each new "friend" with a critical eye, judging them against your idea of who would be the ideal person for your mom or dad (usually your other parent). No doubt this person will be quite different from the person you want them to be with—and that is as it should be. Don't size them up as a future mom or dad. Just accept them

What would you do

if your mother or father decided to get married to someone else?

as you would any of your parent's friends, and get to know them slowly.

But what do you do when a parent gets into a serious relationship, when they decide to marry again, or move in with someone new? Even when you like someone, it can be uncomfortable to learn that they will be living with your parent, and people who seemed okay at first can seem completely different when you realize that they may become part of your new family.

Problem solving

Just when you thought you had more than enough emotions to deal with because of the divorce, a stepfamily can introduce you to a brand-new set of feelings. While you may be happy that your parent has found someone to love and be loved by, the reality of having someone new living with you full-time can be quite different than having someone stopping by the house for a meal or to watch a movie.

If your parents have been divorced a while, you may have become used to a familiar routine with each parent, and when a new person is brought into that group it may

What would it feel like

to be in a stepfamily?

feel as if your parent has less time for you. If your new stepfather is nice—especially if he is nice—you may feel uncomfortable liking him, simply because it feels as if he is taking the place of your real father. It is no surprise that, in fairy tales, the stepmother is usually described as "evil" or "wicked." It can seem as if this one person stands in the way of your dreams

Coping with a new stepfamily can be difficult. You may feel uncomfortable calling a stepfather "Dad," or may not feel close to your stepbrothers and –sisters. Be sure they know what you're feeling and find a relationship that works for all of you.

of a happy reunion between your mom and dad.

The problems can increase when you try to decide what to call your stepmother or stepfather. This is one area where you can take charge and think about what feels comfortable and right to you. It's probably better not to call your stepparent "Mom" or "Dad," even if they ask you to. This person will play a special role in your life, and over time you may feel close enough to them to think of them as a parent, but at the beginning you may wish to call them by their first name or a nickname that confirms a closer relationship.

If you're asked to call them "Mom" or "Dad," you can politely say that you don't feel comfortable doing that yet.

What would you do

if your stepparent asked you to call them "Mom" or "Dad"?

Let the stepparent know that you're glad they're going to be a part of your life, and then ask if it would be all right if you call them by their first name (or another name that feels comfortable to you).

Remember that names can change. As we grow older, nicknames can be outgrown. A boy who used to be known as Billy may now be Bill, or a family's nickname for a tiny baby girl may not suit her when she becomes a teenager. If you are introduced to someone as "Mr. Jones" or "Mrs. Williams" and then they become your stepparent, it may feel awkward to use their first name. Give yourself time to get used to each change in your life—and ask for more time from the people around you if you need it.

Understanding jealousy

It's normal to resent someone new who enters your parent's life. We tend to think of our family as a kind of circle that holds all the members tightly or loosely together. When a stepparent enters that circle, it can feel crowded, as if there is less room—and less love—for everyone else.

But love is not finite. Like all feelings and emotions, love is not something small that has to be divided up into tiny portions to avoid using it all up. Think about something that you enjoy, like music. You may find a song that you really love, that speaks to how you are feeling at that particular moment. Does that mean you will never enjoy another song? Of course not! You may feel differently about different kinds of music or different groups, preferring one for doing homework and another if you're exercising.

That's how love works. When a stepparent enters the family, it doesn't mean that your parent loves you less. It simply means that they have found someone they want to build a life with—a life with you in it.

Blending is for milkshakes, not families

As Will experienced, a parent's remarriage can be especially challenging when a brand-new family is created, not only with a stepparent but also with stepbrothers and stepsisters. Generally, the adults have a romantic idea (taken from television shows and old movies) that all of the children will blend together into one big, happy family. Unfortunately, as you well know, it is not realistic to place a group of kids together and expect them to instantly love each other. Far too often, just the opposite happens.

When stepbrothers and stepsisters come together, the shape of a family does change. You may lose the role you used to have—for example, you might have been an only child, and now have to get used to having other children in the house. You may have been the oldest or the youngest, the only girl among brothers, or the most athletic or the one who earns the best grades. No matter what your "position" was in your old family, with stepbrothers and stepsisters it is probably going to have to change in some way.

The hardest part about creating a new family is how quickly it is supposed to happen. When a parent meets someone new, falls in love, and decides to marry or move in with that person, the parent is looking for a happy ending. But families take time to grow. If you have brothers or sisters, you know that your relationship with them has grown and changed, just as you have grown and changed. Expect your relationship with your stepbrothers and stepsisters to take the same time to grow. There is no such thing as "instant family."

And now there's a baby

When you enter a stepfamily, your circle of family members expands to include a whole new group of people—stepparents, stepbrothers and stepsisters, and possibly even stepgrandparents, stepuncles and –aunts. . . . The list goes on and on. And often, your parent and stepparent may decide to add to this group by having their own baby.

While it is natural for two adults who live together to want to spread their love even further by having a baby, the results may leave some teens wrestling with a lot of different emotions. First might be jealousy. You may feel jealous of the baby, simply because he or she will have both parents full time. You may feel jealous of the baby for not having to deal with all of the results left behind when parents divorce. Let's face it, you may feel jealous of the baby for the same reason all brothers and sisters feel jealous when a baby enters the family: everyone will be fussing and competing for time with the baby, while you're feeling left out and unwanted.

How would you feel

if your parent and stepparent had a baby?

All of these feelings are normal and natural. But get ready for a surprise: chances are that there will be moments when you, too, enjoy the baby. If you're an only child, or the youngest, it can be fun to experience being the big brother or sister. Babies can be a lot of work, and any offer of help you can make will be needed and appreciated by your parent.

The biggest fear many teens report when a new baby enters their divorced family is that they will somehow be "replaced" by the baby. It makes sense to feel this way,

The birth of a new baby in the stepfamily can inspire some painful emotions. You may feel jealous of the attention the new baby receives. It is important to remember that a new child never "replaces" any of the other children in the family.

particularly if the new baby is the same sex as you are. But remember that one person can never replace another, and love for a child is not limited to one son or one daughter. A parent's love can stretch out to make room for many without leaving less for you. And recognize that you have your own unique and special role in your parent's life.

The best advice is to admit your feelings and not be embarrassed about feeling jealous or anxious if a new baby is on the way. If you feel comfortable, share your feelings with your parent. And remember how important your role is in the life of this new baby—you will be part of the baby's family from the moment he or she first enters the world.

A New Start

■ Michelle was completely unprepared when her father said that he would be moving to an apartment. Her parents had had plenty of fights, but so did the parents of all of her friends and they didn't leave. Simply "changing"—the only reason her parents could give her for their decision—didn't seem like enough to tear apart their family. Couldn't they "change" in the same house? She and her brother were changing, and they didn't need to move out of the house to do it. It didn't make sense.

Michelle's strongest feeling that day, and for many days after, was anger. She was furious with her father for moving out, furious with her mother for just standing there and watching him leave without a word of protest, and furious at everybody else whose parents fought and argued much more often than her parents had and yet managed to stay together.

Many teens whose parents have divorced become suspicious or worried about their own futures and the likelihood that

After a family break-up, teens may lose faith in the durability of relationships. It is important to share the many emotions that arise at this stressful time.

their own marriages will end in divorce. They may fear that their children will experience the same pain they felt, and worry that they will make the same mistakes that their parents made.

Teens may be left with a great feeling of insecurity when their basic family structure has collapsed. If a parent has moved in with or married someone else, and that relationship also ended, it is even more likely that teens will feel uncertain about whether or not a marriage can last. They may find it hard to trust others who care for them, find it uncomfortable to date, and feel jealous of friends whose parents are still together.

There are many different emotions that are commonly felt by children whose parents decide to divorce. While we have discussed some ways to solve the problems you may encounter if your parents are divorcing or divorced, it is important to do more than simply solve specific situations or problems—you must also deal with the mixed-up emotions triggered by a divorce. Feelings like anger, depression, fear and anxiety, jealousy . . . these are all normal and natural. There are some practical steps that you can take to help manage these emotions, without denying them or letting them manage you.

How would you feel about marriage if your parents' marriage ended in divorce?

Dealing with feelings

Anger can be a harsh feeling, swirling up suddenly and unexpectedly. As you grow older, you will begin to recognize the things that make you most angry. You will begin to see certain patterns in the times when you feel angry, and understand the areas where you are most sensitive.

Divorce can trigger tremendous amounts of anger. The two people who have decided to divorce will inevitably be angry at each other, while they are divorcing and often for years after the divorce. They are angry at each other for the words and actions that have sparked the divorce, but also angry at the loss of a dream—the dream of a future lived happily ever after.

Their children have a right to feel angry, as well. They have also lost a dream of a happy future, lived with two parents together in one home. They are now forced to change their lives in order to cope with the divorce.

What steps would you take to move beyond your parents' divorce?

At times, understanding can be the first step in managing your anger. It may help to talk to your parents and ask them to explain the reasons for the divorce. Ask them to be specific. Be honest about your own feelings. Admit your anger. Let them know that the divorce has made things difficult for you. Be clear in your need for information. If your parents are comfortable sharing the circumstances of the divorce with you, you may gain some information that will help you understand why the divorce happened.

If the thought of sharing your feelings openly with your parents is too scary, try writing them down. Keep a journal, and write in it when you are feeling angry or upset. Putting your feelings down on paper will help you to understand the times and situations when you are most angry, and also will give you a safe place to let go of those strong emotions. Or write a letter to your parents—a letter that you may never decide to give them, but a letter that honestly explains your feelings and gives you a way to put down on paper the questions or feelings that you would like to, one day, express.

Anger can create a tremendous amount of energy. You want to be able to direct that energy into a positive, rather than negative, force. In addition to releasing your anger by speaking it or writing it down, you may find that physical activities are a positive outlet for strong emotions. Sports are a great way to channel energy, whether you choose a team sport like football, soccer, or field hockey, or a competitive sport like swimming or running.

Managing depression

Depression can be a deadly emotion, robbing you of energy and enthusiasm. It is important to recognize depression and to take steps to manage it.

Depression is a feeling of deep and lasting sadness, a sense of disappointment in life. For teens dealing with divorced parents, this feeling often follows significant events or holidays—times when families should be coming together

The depression that often accompanies a family break-up can be a difficult challenge, especially for teens. It is important that teens recognize the signs of depression and take steps to treat this often severe condition.

to celebrate. When parents have divorced, their children often feel as if their parents' needs must always come first. Times that should be special for their children turn into a balancing act to meet each parent's demands. Children often wrestle with guilt, feeling uncomfortable if they are having too much fun with one parent, as if that fun somehow comes at the expense of the other parent. They may feel guilty for liking a new stepparent, feel guilty for enjoying a vacation, even feel guilty when a "family" picture is taken with new relatives. And feeling guilty about enjoying yourself can quickly lead to sadness, and then depression.

Depression's greatest power is its ability to turn the world into a gray place, as if it were shutting doors and windows and closing out all the sources of light. It is important to fight back, to not allow yourself to be closed into a sad place. The first and best thing you can do is to force yourself to keep moving, to continue to do the things that normally make you happy, even when you don't want to. If you enjoy being outdoors, go outside for a walk or a run. If you feel better with friends, call them and arrange to meet somewhere. The important thing is to hold on to the things that make you happy and continue to do them, even when your energy level is low.

Remember that this feeling, like all feelings, is temporary. The situation that caused you to feel sad is also temporary. If you are feeling helpless because of the actions of the adults in your life, remember that you, too, will soon be an adult and be able to make your own decisions about where and how you want to live. While you are not responsible for the circum-

Would you feel comfortable discussing your feelings about your parents' divorce with a counselor?

stances of your life, you are responsible for how you react to them. Choose not to be overwhelmed, but instead find the things that make you happy and hold onto them. Look for friends, for people who make you feel good about yourself, and spend time with them.

Be honest about the way you feel. If one parent is saying unkind things about the other, or criticizing him or her, let them know that it makes you sad to hear these things. Ask them not to criticize the other parent when you are there. If they are asking you to carry messages to the other parent and this makes you uncomfortable, let them know. Tell them that they need to speak to each other directly, not through you.

If you are finding it difficult to do the things you want to do because of custody arrangements or visitation schedules, let both parents know. Be honest about what you would like to do. Explain that a particular sport requires a certain practice schedule, or that you want to spend Saturdays participating in a particular activity. Do not feel that you have to come up with a solution. Let both parents know what the conflict is, and then let them work it out together.

One final thought about depression—we often feel better ourselves when we can help someone else. If you have brothers or sisters, recognize that they will also be suffering because of the divorce. Remember that you may be experiencing similar feelings, or worrying about similar problems. Be honest with them about your feelings, and listen to theirs. Brothers and sisters can offer each other a powerful source of support as their family struggles with divorce.

Overcoming fear

The unknown can be a source of great anxiety and stress, and for children whose parents are divorcing, there is much that is unknown. Where will I live? When will I spend time with Mom, and when will I spend time with Dad? What will happen on holidays? Will I have to change schools? The future can be full of question marks, and this uncertainty can be particularly painful when a family breaks apart and children are caught in the middle.

The first step lies in simply admitting what frightens you. Say it out loud, or write it down. Be honest about what most worries you about the divorce. You may be worried that you won't be able to handle certain situations without both parents to support you. You may worry about not seeing your mother or father. You may worry that, when a parent decides to remarry, an important part of your life will be erased.

Whatever it is that frightens you, be honest about it. Share your questions with your parents. Ask them to explain how different situations will be handled. Ask them to commit to a

Uncertainty over the future after a divorce can lead to fear and jealousy. It is important to remember you are not alone. Share your feelings at these times — both with family members and friends.

visitation schedule, or to plan a time each day when they will phone you. Do not feel that you need to face your fears alone. Ask your parents to face them with you.

Dealing with jealousy

Jealousy is often a mixed-up stew of lots of other feelings: anger, insecurity, fear, and disappointment. Jealousy is what you feel when something you have is taken away from you. For this reason, jealousy is often triggered when your parent begins to date after the divorce, when they decide to remarry, or when stepbrothers or stepsisters enter your family. It can be difficult to share a parent's attention or time, particularly if custody arrangements limit you to only a small amount of that time and attention each week.

Understanding jealousy is often an important step in managing it. Examine exactly why you are feeling jealous.

Often we direct our anger and jealousy at a particular person—a new baby, a new stepparent—when, in fact, it is a parent who is at the heart of the problem. If you need more time with a parent, if you are feeling excluded from their new life, be honest with them. Share you feelings. Ask them if it would be possible to have more one-on-one time with them, or to schedule a regular event that is just for the two of you.

Remember that all new relationships take time. There is no such thing as an instant family. And emotions can creep up unexpectedly, presenting new challenges all the time. Be honest with your feelings, and patient while waiting for situations to change.

What the future holds

While a parents' divorce can be shattering, it should not become the defining point of a teen's life. There are many ways to move past the pain of your parent's divorce, to become stronger and more comfortable with the shape your family has taken—a shape perhaps different than the neat circle you would have wished for, but a shape large enough to fit many different people and new kinds of relationships.

In this book, we have discussed the initial pain of a divorce and ways to handle the changes in family life. We have talked about custody and visits with parents, and how to minimize the problems that can occur when you're moving between two homes. We have examined the difficulties of having only one parent involved in your life, and what you might do if a parent wishes to step back into your life after a long absence. We have talked about the joys and hassles of stepfamilies and how to handle being in one.

Would you like to join a support group for teens whose parents had divorced?

As this book makes clear, a divorce comes in different forms depending on the relationship parents are able to build with their former spouse and with their children after the marriage has ended. Children of divorced parents can find themselves in many different circumstances, but they all need to develop two important skills: honesty (talking openly with their parents) and flexibility (being willing to accept change and find ways to work through it).

Part of the challenge of growing up is selecting what works and what doesn't—and making choices based on those selections. We choose how to live our lives based in part on our experiences—seeing where we've succeeded and failed and learning from those successes and failures— and also on the experiences of the people around us. Lessons in love, relationships, and marriage come first from our parents. If they find someone to care for, if they build a lasting relationship and live "happily ever after," then we can take with us the knowledge that marriages can succeed with hard work and smart choices.

If your parents did not succeed at "happily ever after" with each other, will this prevent you from ever building a successful marriage? Of course not. It simply means that you need to learn from their experiences, as well as the experiences of other people.

If your parents are comfortable talking about their marriage, and you feel comfortable talking with them about it, you might want to ask them why they think the marriage did not work. Ask them for specifics, rather than something like, "we wanted different things," or "we grew apart." Perhaps

> **What would you want** to do differently to make sure that you did not experience another divorce?

they might share something like, "we married too young,"

or "we didn't really get to know each other before we got married."

As young people begin to explore different careers, they are often encouraged to look for a *mentor*, someone who is skilled at that particular job or trade and can share their experiences with a person just starting out. They can be valuable resources for the positives and negatives of a particular job, with ideas about how to succeed and also with cautions about things to avoid.

The same approach can help you if you are anxious about the prospects for your own future. Find someone you trust and admire whose marriage has worked—one that has lasted for several years. Ask them how they did it, and what advice they can share. You will find, if you talk to more than one person, that their stories will have certain points in common, and from those points you can begin to build a framework that will help you go forward to create your own happy marriage in the future.

Call it courage

When you have suffered through a divorce, you have experienced a pain that children whose parents are still together cannot know. The family that brought you into the world has vanished, and you are left with something quite different. You may be left with only one parent actively involved in your life. You may be left with a back-and-forth schedule between two homes that means you're never where you want to be at any particular time. You may find yourself caught in the middle between two adults still fighting long after their divorce has been finalized.

These are not easy issues to deal with. But you should know that you are not alone. With nearly half of all marriages ending in divorce, with 25 percent of all American children spending time in a stepfamily, there

Part of growing up is learning what works and what doesn't. Rebuilding family relationships after a divorce does present some tough challenges—but it can create some valuable learning opportunities as well.

clearly are many other teens struggling with some of the same feelings of anger, confusion, and sadness that you may be experiencing.

It takes great courage to move beyond a great sadness. It takes courage to be honest with others about your feelings, to share your disappointment, your anger, and your fear. When your parents divorce, you will struggle with many changes. There are no easy answers or quick solutions for what comes next. Mistakes will be made—by you and your parents. But with hard work and honesty, you can step beyond your parents' divorce towards your own happy ending.

Glossary

Alimony – money given by the spouse who earns more to his or her husband or wife for a certain time period after the divorce.

Assets – the property a married couple owns that must be divided during a divorce.

At-home bag – a bag a child of divorce can pack with his or her favorite things, to make them feel at home no matter where they are.

Child support – money given by one parent to another to help support their children after a divorce.

Custody – the legal right to take care of a child and make important decisions that will affect him or her.

Decree – the legal document that spells out the terms of the divorce.

Depression – a feeling of deep and lasting sadness that can rob the sufferer of energy and enthusiasm.

Divorce – a legal document that ends a marriage.

Joint custody – an agreement between divorced parents to share the responsibility for the care and support of their children.

Visitation – a document that creates a schedule of when and for how long a child will visit each parent after a divorce.

Further Reading

Books:

Bonkowski, Sara. *Teens are Non-Divorceable*. Chicago, IL: ACTA Publications, 1990.

Danziger, Paula. *Amber Brown is Feeling Blue*. New York: G.P. Putnam's Sons, 1998.

Gardner, Richard A. *The Boys and Girls Book About Divorce*. New York: Bantam, 1985.

Holyoke, Nancy. *Help! A Girl's Guide to Divorce and Stepfamilies*. Middleton, WI: Pleasant Co., 1999.

Krementz, Jill. *How It Feels When Parents Divorce*. New York: Alfred A. Knopf. 1988.

Web sites:

www.kidexchange.about.com

www.kidshealth.org

www.kidsinthemiddle.org

www.kidsturn.org

www.mytwohomes.com

www.stepfamily.net

Index

Alimony, decisions about
in divorce decree, 6, 10
Assets, decisions about in
divorce decree, 6, 7, 10
At-Home Bag, 27-28
Attorney/lawyer, 7, 10
Birthdays, parental
involvement in after
divorce, 29, 31
Children of divorcing
parents
and avoiding getting
caught in the middle
of parents, 9, 21-23,
29-31, 36, 53
and courage, 58-59
and flexibility, 57
and honesty, 20, 30-31,
33, 39, 51, 53-54, 56,
57, 59
and identity issues,
17-19
journals kept by, 51, 54
number of, 12, 58-59
and physical activities,
51, 53
and responsibility for
divorce, 19
See also Feelings, of
children of divorcing
parents
Child support
decisions about in
divorce decree, 6-7, 10
parent having difficulty
paying, 36
Custody, 24-33
and At-Home Bag,
27-28

and beginning of visits,
26-27
and birthdays, 29, 31
and child's conflicts
with schdedule, 53-54
and child's role in deci-
sion on, 31-33
decisions about in
divorce decree, 7, 10
definition of, 7, 10, 25
and different parenting
styles, 28-29
and jealousy, 55
joint, 25-26
parental conflict over
after divorce, 12
and parental involvement
in big, unscheduled
events, 7, 12, 29-31
See also Visitation
Decree, 7, 10-11, 13
Divorce
and decree, 7, 10-11, 13
definition of, 6-7, 9-11
as ending and beginning,
7, 11-13
family continuing after,
7, 12, 13
prevalence of, 6, 9, 21
reasons for, 19-20
terms of, 6-7, 10
Feelings, of children of
divorcing parents, 48-59
anger, 16, 20, 39, 50-51,
59
anxiety about own
marriage, 48-49, 50,
57-58
bargaining, 16, 19-20

denial, 16
depression, 16, 50,
51-54
fear, 50, 54-55, 59
guilt, 26, 52
insecurity, 17-19, 49
jealousy, 44-45, 46-47,
49, 50, 55-56
and mentor easing fears
of own marriage, 58
pain, 6, 10, 17
sharing of, 20-21, 54, 59
toward stepfamily,
42-43, 44-45, 46-47,
55, 56
Finances
conflicts about after
divorce, 12
decisions about in
divorce decree, 6,
7, 10
Joint custody, 25-26
See also Custody
Kübler-Ross, Elisabeth,
16
Mother, employment of
after divorce, 7, 12
Moving, after divorce,
7, 12
School events, parental
involvement in after
divorce, 7, 12, 29-31
Single parent, 34-39
child scheduling visit
with, 36-38
child's reunion with,
38-39
and child support diffi-
culties, 36

reasons for absence of,
34-36
sense of shame and
failure of, 34-35
Stepfamily, 40-47
and dating by parents,
41-42, 55
and end of fantasy of
family reunion, 40-41,
42-43
and feelings toward
stepparent, 42-43

and jealousy and love,
44-45, 46-47, 55, 56
and name for stepparent,
43-44
and new baby, 46-47,
56
and stepbrothers and
stepsisters, 37,
45-46, 55
Visitation
and beginning of visits,
26-27

child's awareness of
schedule for, 27
decisions about in divorce
decree, 7, 10, 26
definition of, 25
parents committing
to schedule for, 20,
54-55
parents late for, 27
parents postponing, 27
parents upset about, 26
See also Custody

About the Author

Heather Lehr Wagner is a writer and editor. She is the author of several books for teens, including *Blending Foster and Adopted Children into the Family* and *Dealing with Terminal Illness in the Family* in the Focus on Family Matters series.

About the Editor

Marvin Rosen is a licensed clinical psychologist who practices in Media, Pennsylvania. He received his doctorate degree from the University of Pennsylvania in 1961. Since 1963, he has worked with intellectually and emotionally challenged people at Elwyn, Inc. in Pennsylvania, with clinical, administrative, research, and training responsibilities. He also conducts a private practice of psychology. Dr. Rosen has taught psychology at the University of Pennsylvania, Bryn Mawr College, and West Chester University. He has written or edited seven book and numerous professional articles in the areas of psychology, rehabilitation, emotional disturbance, and mental retardation.